HOW TO BE A
BADASS

A Survival Guide For Women

Sharon Law Tucker

How To Be A BadAss – A Survival Guide For Women
Copyright © 2015 Sharon Law Tucker

www.BadAssWoman.com

ISBN#13: 9781517544898
ISBN#10: 1517544890

Three Gals Publishing

Three Gals Publishing™
inspiring genius©

Dedication

In memory of Richard Syre Tucker, beloved husband and teacher; the wisest man I ever knew.

*You just never know what's going to help
you at some future point. So whatever
it is, approach it as if it's the most important
thing you will do in your life because, at that
moment, it is.*

Foreword

I have known Sharon for the past two years, and in those two years she has taken me under her wing and helped guide me into my twenties both professionally and as a friend and mentor. I can't remember exactly when, but she was telling one of (many) badass stories, and when she concluded I promptly turned to her and said, "Sharon, you need to write all of this into a book." We agreed that everything she had shared with me as a young woman was so valuable and pertinent that other women no matter their age could also benefit from her experiences. The book she has so diligently prepared is loaded with anecdotes, aphorisms, and the collective wisdom of her experiences. I can tell you that what lies ahead in this book are the ingredients to becoming a badass which they don't teach in school, or which you cannot necessarily find on the internet. Much of the information in the book may come off as common sense, or no brainers to some people, but as a young woman trying to push through the glass ceiling, and as someone who attends an all-women's college I routinely see that what's offered in this book is needed now more than ever for women. No matter what your occupation, personality, or prowess, there's at least a little bit of a badass inside of us all.

Therese M. Soares
Student
Mills College

Recipe for a BadAss Woman

I've known Sharon for many years and when she shared with me she aspired to write this book, I could not help but to want to be a part of it. This book is filled with the truths of Sharon and I wanted to add a tribute to her wisdom, courage and faith. Additionally, I wanted to offer something to help you know and understand Sharon as I do.

So, Sharon, I dedicate to you this recipe as it truly reflects who you are. Thank you for being the BadAss Woman that you are and helping me become the BadAss Woman that I am. I am. That I am.

Glad to know ya!
Your Gal Pal, Sheila

How to Be a BadAss Recipe

A DASH OF BITTERS *(required for the times when you have to be a bitch)*

¼ CUP OF COMMON SENSE *(for choosing your paths wisely)*

A SPOONFUL OF HONEY *(for acknowledging the good in others)*

1 oz of FLEXIBILITY *(for when going with the flow is the obvious choice)*

6 cups of COURAGE *(for living YOUR truth)*

2 HEAPING CUPS OF TRUE GRIT *(for getting through the tough times)*

A SPLASH OF SPIRITUALITY *(for keeping the faith in knowing you are not alone)*

1 cup of KICK ASS *(to remind difficult people you are not a doormat)*

AND A WHOLE LOTTA INTEGRITY *(for when you look in the mirror, you like the person you see)*

Serving instructions: Take it in sips ladies, as you will need it to last a lifetime!

- Sheila Shaw

Introduction

We are born into this life with a clean slate. No imprints or presupposed ideas. Those come with time and experience born out of the relationships we have with our parents, brothers and sisters, friends and neighbors, pastors, teachers and everyone else telling us how to live, how to think, how to feel, how to be, how to act, how to express ourselves or not; basically, to be good little girls and follow the rules. Some of us survive and some of us become victims...until now.

Failure is not personal. It's just a lesson to help you be successful next time.

Contents

Cows Are Not Bulls and Women Are Not Men

I love my husband. He was a wonderful, amazing man and my best friend. But he was not a woman. As women, we need women friends in our lives to complement the feminine side of our nature: that special warmth, love, affection and understanding that only women can give other women. This is not about being straight, lesbian or bisexual. It's about that feminine bond that makes us women whether we're gay or straight. It's that special something that binds us together in a crisis, and helps us to understand the pain and loss that we experience in life in the same way. Women understand each other's grief and joy; men handle these things in a very different way.

Don't expect to turn a man into a woman and don't try to turn a woman into a man. You'll

Sharon Law Tucker

be disappointed. A lot of women attempt to do this without realizing it and wind up alienating their husbands and never understand why their husbands can't make them happy.

Instead, celebrate the differences and draw from both to round out your life and emotional needs. And if you find that you prefer not to have a man in your life, that's perfectly okay too. As women, we have feminine and masculine sides of our nature that define who we are. The fortunate are able to find that which complements their nature to round out who they are. The less fortunate never come to terms.

I'm not a trained counselor or psychologist, but it's been my experience that when confronted with a difficult situation or loss, men withdraw and women need to talk. If you figure this out, you just might survive together through all the ups and downs you'll face over the years. Appreciate the differences as you reach out to your women friends and counselors, giving your husband or partner time and space, and after a time of emotional separation, you just may find your way back to each other. There's no guarantee in a situation like this as each man is different. But if his period of withdrawal or emotional separation goes on too long, counseling may be necessary.

*Don't expect to turn a man into a woman
and don't try to turn a woman into
a man. You'll be disappointed.*

2

Never Eat a Cold Burger

This may seem elemental for some of you, but if you order a burger rare and it comes back medium-rare, you have a decision to make as to whether or not to eat it. Chances are you'll say, oh darn, and eat it anyway, and that's perfectly okay as long as you make a conscious decision to do so. However, if it comes back well-done, don't hesitate to send it back. If you're paying for it, you should have it the way you want it.

When I was a young woman, the thought of sending a steak back to be cooked properly never occurred to me. Never had I seen anyone in our family send anything back to be prepared to her satisfaction. We always ate what was put before us.

Then I met my husband. If his steak wasn't cooked until it was dead, done and brown all the way through, he'd send it back. The first

5

time it happened, I looked at him and said, "You can do that?" "Of course," he replied, "I want it the way I want it." What a novel idea.

I had a girlfriend who loved to buy new clothes and would go shopping at least once a month. But she hated to try on dresses at the store. So she'd pick out eight to ten outfits, bring them home, and try them on, picking out the right shoes and accessories until she found just the perfect ensemble. This was a procedure that could take all day so quite often she'd save this for a Saturday and invite me over. We would drink wine and make an event of it. After selecting two or three perfect outfits, she'd take the rest back and get credit for the returned items. I'm sure the clerks dreaded seeing her coming but she bought a lot of clothes over time.

It never occurred to me to return an item that didn't fit right or I had a change of mind. The only time I returned an item was if it was damaged in some way. To think that I could return something just because it didn't match my eyes wasn't in my thought process, but learning from her, if I changed my mind because I bought something on impulse (which I've been known to do on occasion), I now take it back. I'm in charge of my life and it feels great!

Learning to know what you want and say it right out loud is a pretty recent luxury for women. A few years ago women were taught to do what they were told, be the good little woman, and in many cases not only were they trained to keep their opinions to themselves, but they were used to someone else doing the thinking for them and quite often didn't even know what they thought or what they liked.

Many women were used to a father or husband doing the thinking and making all the decisions for them and the entire family. The Women's Movement brought about major changes for women and today more and more women are not suppressed. Unfortunately, there are still women who feel shy about expressing themselves or having an opinion about anything.

Years ago there was a great movie called *Tootsie* with Dustin Hoffman and Teri Garr.

There is one scene where Teri's character says, "I read *The Cinderella Complex*. I know I'm responsible for my own orgasm." That pretty well sums it up. If you want to be happy and in charge of your life, then take control to get what you want and don't settle for something less because you're too shy or embarrassed to try. The key is to speak up. Don't hold back. You've really got nothing to lose by saying you want something your way. The worst thing that can happen is you will be told no. Oh darn!

If a Frog Had Wings He Wouldn't Bump His Ass When He Hopped

This old country saying has a lot of wisdom hidden in it. We hear "ifs" all day long. If I could do this or if I had only done that. Don't waste your time worrying about what you coulda shoulda woulda done in a situation. If you didn't take advantage of an opportunity, a chance was missed. So what! Just make it a point not to hesitate the next time. Grab it and growl. If you made a wrong decision, learn from it so you don't repeat it next time.

Mistakes are lessons. As long as you learn from a mistake, then it wasn't wasted. If you waste the lesson, that's the crime, not the mistake. Learn, grow and be better, or do it better next time then move on. "IF" is an excuse if you constantly use it. Badass women don't make excuses. They learn!

Are Diamonds in Your Backyard?

One of the first books Richard introduced me to was *Psycho-Pictography*, written by Vernon Howard. It used mental pictures or parables to make a point. This book had a profound effect on me over the years. One story was titled, "Look for Diamonds in Your Own Backyard." In other words, quite often the solution to a problem may be right under your nose or as far away as your backyard.

As a young woman, I was always looking to be "saved" by someone outside my immediate sphere. I was looking for help, a solution, wealth, an idea, love, etc., from anyone who might pass by instead of relying on myself. No matter what the situation, the answer was always out there somewhere else.

For example, when I was a teenager I was always looking for ways to make money. I grew up near Big Sur. My parents were part owners of a 4,000-acre ranch with hills and streams covered with a bounty of scents and aromas from all kinds of herbs, trees and bushes. Bay laurel trees flourished along with sage, rosemary and wild lilac. It was a step into heaven just taking a hike in the back hills. My stepfather said repeatedly, "Why don't you make sachets and sell them to tourists?" It was so simple I let it pass. A few years later, people were making fortunes farming and selling, you guessed it, sachets from local flora. That's one lesson I never forgot. The moral of that story is, the answer to a problem could be staring you right in the face and it's so close, you won't see it. Start looking around you for simple answers to your problems instead of always looking outside.

Never Leave Money
on the Table

Learn to negotiate, negotiate, negotiate. The art of negotiating is a talent and one of my friends has perfected it to an art. This is a woman you want with you when you're buying a car or negotiating the purchase of a house. She raised and traded horses and developed a talent she now uses anytime she's out to make a purchase.

As women, we bargain hunt at Macy's or Nordstrom's and that's great. Now take it to the next level and learn to ask for a deal. Don't accept the face value price of something just because it's there. Most things, especially big-ticket items, are negotiable. Learn this art and believe me, the sales people will hate to see you coming but your bank account will thank you and you will save thousands of dollars over the course of a lifetime.

And if they are tight with the dinner tab,
they'll be tight with you!

Frugal Is Not Cheap

A number of years ago there was a wonderful TV chef, Jeff Smith, who called himself the Frugal Gourmet. He was all about buying quality cuts of meat and fine ingredients but without waste. That was what frugal meant to him and I like that definition.

Being frugal is smart. It means you handle your finances wisely and make careful decisions to spend your money on things that really matter. It means getting value for dollar. It does not mean being cheap. Nobody likes or respects a cheapskate. (Just watch how some men keep their wallet close to their chest when they pay a dinner tab and eke out a whopping 10% tip. *And if they are tight with the dinner tab, they'll be tight with you!)*

My friend and neighbor is retired, loves to enjoy fine dining, and plans for these occasions. However, she watches for sales and if there is a deal for something she can use, she doesn't miss very many. She saves 2-for-1 coupons for things she needs and looks for special deals for things she can use. This is being frugal...not cheap. She's generous, giving and caring of herself, and if you need help, she's there. A true friend. She knows that with the few dollars she saves, she's free to enjoy the things that give her the greatest pleasure, like going to dinner with me. Whoopee!! I've learned a lot from her.

Richard and I set up piggy banks in the house to collect savings from coupons or from those special sales or discounts (Richard was great for saying "how much did we save today?") and when we saved enough, we'd go to dinner or a movie or buy something we needed. Back in the day, these savings would add up and we would take the savings to buy tires for the car or that important brake job. We never missed the money while we were saving.

Don't Try to Turn a Caterpillar into a Frog

Caterpillars are best left to be caterpillars and when they are allowed to do what comes naturally, you just might get a butterfly. Wanting the best for your loved one or wanting to help someone become the best they can be is a noble cause. However, it's important that you approach this cautiously, without attempting to transform them into something they are not. Don't ever think you're going to change someone. *The power to change comes from within and they have to want to change. Instead, be a role model and encourage by example.* Motivate, don't dictate.

I knew a woman who fell madly in love with a man she thought she could make over. The man she married was everything she wanted except when it came to his profession. In that aspect, he wasn't the man she thought she wanted and so in her mind, she created the perfect man, the perfect husband. He was very good-looking and kind, with a good heart and a good job. She hounded him to get more education, take night classes, and in her words, become something. She pushed and pushed and pushed and for a time, he did what she wanted.

But eventually, after feeling brow-beaten and worthless and tired of trying to live up to her expectations, he got fed up and asked for a divorce. She was stunned. She couldn't believe he was unhappy. She only wanted the best for him and for herself. What was wrong?

The problem was the man was a mechanic and loved being a mechanic and never wanted to be anything else. His wife kept pushing him to take classes in business administration because she thought he was smart and capable of so much more and that he merely lacked ambition and confidence in his abilities. He saw her as being pushy and not respecting him for who and what he was and that she disapproved or was disappointed in him.

It wasn't until the marriage was pushed to the breaking point that they sat down to figure out where the disconnect was. His problem was he didn't want to disappoint her and her problem was she had unrealistic expectations of him. She wasn't looking at him for who he was or what he wanted to do, but what in her mind he could become. It's great to encourage and support each other but make sure you're supporting and encouraging someone for the right reasons and not your own agenda. When I review this story, it appears to me that she should have gone to school and become the business executive and he would have been as proud as he could be to support her. Projecting your wants or dreams onto another person will eventually lead to problems unless that person wants them too. Be in charge of your own destiny and let others be free to do the same.

The power to change comes from within and they have to want to change. Instead, be a role model and encourage by example.

Power Comes to Those Who Take It

Gloria Steinem, godmother of the women's movement in the 1970s, said "Power may be taken, but not given". She went on to say, "The process of taking is empowerment itself." I believe it's more than that. People who have power don't want to give it up. They don't want to share power and they certainly don't want you to have power. So it's up to you to seize the moment. And when you do, if done correctly (it's all about timing and opportunity), you will be respected for it. *Learning to have the confidence to grab the opportunity when it presents itself makes you a winner.* Standing back, waiting for someone to recognize how brilliant or talented you are, or what a great person you are, is going to keep you waiting in the wings forever. If you are passed over for a promotion and you know you are the most qualified person for the job, ask your boss, "I'm deserving, I'm qualified! Why can't I have this promotion?" You may get fired, but on the other hand you just might wind up with a promotion that would have gone to someone else had you not stood up for yourself.

A few years ago I read a story about a young woman working in a large corporation who was being considered for a promotion. She was up against two others who happened to be men; however, she was the more qualified. The story goes that when it came time for the results, the job was going to one of the men. Upset, she leaned across the boardroom table and asked her boss, "Why the hell can't I have it?" referring to the promotion. The result was, she got the job.

Our society today has no respect for shrinking violets. It's the blood-red rose, thorns and all, that grabs attention, but be prepared. After you've got it, you've got to keep it. You've got to back it up with performance so you better be well prepared.

9

How to Be a BadAss Without Being an Asshole

I watched a movie recently with Jack Nicholson called *The Last Detail.* His character called himself a badass and he was, but he was also obnoxious and arrogant. No one likes a self-absorbed, condescending, conceited person. However, taking command of yourself, and not selling yourself short in any given situation, facing challenges head-on instead of hiding out in a locked room, knowing how to accept defeat, such as a job layoff, as a temporary nuisance, and preparing for the next day as a new horizon—now that's a badass worth admiring. It's about being able to look at the Devil and spit in his eye. That's not to say you're not going to feel beaten sometimes; we all do periodically. But when you pick yourself up and go back out there and face that challenge, when you feel your inner core willing to fight back no matter how scared

you are, that's when you are a genuine
badass.

10

Believe in Yourself, and Know You May Need Help Flying

Don't be limited by your limitations. You may have a great idea and possess certain skills or talents that can propel you to success. However, it's realistic to know what you can and can't do, then figure out how to develop skills that will move you forward or figure whom you can turn to for support or to fulfill your vision. There's no such thing as "I Can't," just "How Can I." You may need to do research, find alternatives, get training in certain areas where you are lacking, or reach out to other people. The point is, if you have a great idea and believe it is doable, why not do it?

Most of all, don't let fear of success keep you from succeeding. That was a hard concept for me to understand. I always thought I had a fear of failure, when in fact, it was my fear of being seen as stupid or dumb that held me back. Early in our relationship my husband asked, "What's the worst thing that could happen?" I replied, "I could fail," at which point he replied, "And then what would happen?" I stopped, thought and replied, "I don't know!" He said, "You try again!" It never occurred to me to try again. For me, the idea of failing was so demoralizing that I would rather not do anything than to get an "F" on a report card, or have to do something over until I got it right.

Don't let this kind of thinking stop you from becoming the very best you can be. Thomas Edison spent years working to develop the electric light. Once, he was asked how he could continue after experiencing failure after failure, and his classic reply: "I've not failed, I just found ten thousand ways that won't work." In his lifetime, Edison acquired 10,098 patents. He never stopped believing in himself. He never quit. And keep in mind no one ever talks about his failures.

Never give up trying for your dream. The worst thing that could happen is you learn what doesn't work and you get to try again, only better.

It's common for those of us who have experienced difficulties to want to pass the blame on to someone else or a bad situation. There may actually be some validity in that thinking, but it's important not to use it as an excuse for not taking action or control of your life. It's important to put the skids on blaming your childhood, your parents, or the world for all the ills in your life. Although there is some comfort in that, that kind of thinking will keep you from moving forward. You have one life to live, live it. Never repeat the mistakes of your parents and make sure you're not living someone else's failures. A Chinese proverb by Lao Tzu says, "A journey of a thousand miles begins with a single step." START NOW!

Learning to have the confidence to grab the opportunity when it presents itself makes you a winner.

11

Life Is a Banquet.
Go Take Your Fill!

Oprah Winfrey suffered a terrible childhood of abuse and was repeatedly molested by family members from the age of 9 to 13. I'm sure that experience is no faint memory for her, but I don't think there's anyone within earshot of a TV that doesn't know her success story. She sets a shining example to us all as to what can be overcome when you believe in yourself and work at it. Oprah said, "It doesn't matter who you are, where you came from. The ability to triumph begins with you. Always." Great words to live by and to never forget. Life is about choice. Your choice. Choose wisely.

The high-maintenance friend is typically a controller and requires accounting for every misstep in your life.

12

High Maintenance Vs. Low Maintenance Friendships

We are each in our own way busy trying to survive the daily pressures of life. Whether we are workers or mothers, students or entrepreneurs, we are each in our own way trying to survive the rigors of getting through each and every day. And hopefully, one day, we will find at least some measure of joy. That is the payoff for a life well lived.

One of the basic lessons I learned was to surround myself with low-maintenance friendships. These are friends who can ebb* and flow with the changes that take place in your life as well as theirs. If you schedule a lunch date and have to cancel, no problem, you schedule for another day. A simple explanation should be enough. However, I've known a few people who completely unravel at any change in their schedule and a simple request to make a change or move a date is a major catastrophe.

My feeling is that it's important to be flexible and respectful and allow for those unexpected life situations that may be an inconvenience but are not life-or-death situations. You are there for each other, to support each other, and in a crisis, you will do whatever it takes to be there for that person, and she (hopefully) will be there for you.

High-maintenance friends are demanding and if there is an unexpected change, while they may be understanding, they'll never let an opportunity pass without making you feel guilty. I once had a friend with whom I normally talked once a week. Something happened and a week went by. I received one of those "we have to talk" calls, which just curls my toes and immediately puts me on the defensive, instead of a message like, "Hey, I haven't heard from you, are you all right? Do you need anything? I hope you're making a ton of money and having a great time. Give me a call when you come up for air." That's a friend. A real friend.

I'm not saying a high-maintenance friend can't be a real friend too, but you can't afford too many of these in your life. They're just too demanding of your time and energy. *The high-maintenance friend is typically a controller and requires accounting for every misstep in your life.* The point is, be selective. At first it's very flattering to think that somebody misses you that much. Over time at some point, this type of friend may find some reason to turn on you. This is their defense mechanism for handling their loss of control, and if they mean something to you and it doesn't take too much out of you then enjoy them for as long as it works for you. Usually these people just want to be reassured that they're still important to you. So if you have a person like this in your life, enjoy them for who they are and the fun times you have together. However, when they pull the rug out from under you, know that you will have a choice to "prove yourself," or just be ready to walk away.

My friend was just like this. She was so much fun, and funny too. She could have been a standup comedian. We were friends for about four years. When I didn't do just the right thing or say exactly what she thought I should say by following some perfectly conceived script she had written in her head, then the sky would fall. Frankly, I just got tired of the drama. She had no idea how ill my husband was at the time and some of the financial burdens that hit me at that point. And she never asked. All she cared about was I hadn't called her in a week. For me, I just couldn't deal with it anymore. It took too much out of me to continue the relationship with everything else that was going on in my life.

This is a decision only you can make. These people have some real issues and should seek counseling. They like to be the one to walk away from a relationship first so as to avoid being rejected. Just know this and do not take on the responsibility of their happiness. It's their problem and they're the ones who need you more than you need them.

Don't Try to Lift a Two-Ton Boulder

You can't change a person to become what you want them to become, nor should you try to mold yourself into someone else's idea of perfection. We do the very best we can, the best we are capable of at any given time or situation, and sometimes it's just not enough. But enough for who?

There was a time when I was really struggling with what I thought was someone's betrayal of my trust. It was killing me. I just couldn't understand how this person could have done this to me. I was devastated and couldn't come to terms with it. My best friend and I decided to go have drinks at Spanish Bay Inn on the beautiful 17-Mile Drive, listen to the bagpiper play and watch the sun set. As we were walking back to my car, my friend, who had gone through years of therapy, stopped me and said, "Sharon, go pick up that two-ton boulder." I laughed and said, "Don't be ridiculous!" She said, "I'm serious. Go pick it up." I replied, "You know I can't." And she knowingly replied, "That's right. And neither can she. She did what she did because she couldn't do anything else at the time. We can only do what we are capable of. Each of us has our limitations. It doesn't make her bad or good, it's just who she is. You need to let it go."

This was an aha! moment for me. I've thought about this again and again over the years and found this lesson to be one of the most profound I've since incorporated in my life. It just might save you a lot of grief. Not everyone has your sense of right or wrong, or puts the same value on your friendship that you do. That's just the way it is. When you expect someone to meet your standards and then feel betrayed when they don't, it is probably more about you than it is about them. Putting high expectations on casual or even close friends will most likely cause you grief. Save this for your significant other or spouse and even then, make allowances if people don't live up to your ideal of perfection. After all, you probably don't live up to their ideal either. And for all the rest, just take them as a gift for as long as it can last.

One of my favorite movies is *Teahouse of the August Moon*. It takes place in Okinawa after World War II. In it Glenn Ford's character is a man who never seems to be able to accomplish anything and everything he touches turns to mud. At one point, he made the reflection upon his life, "I've come to terms between my aspirations and my limitations." I've always thought that was an extremely important lesson. *It took me many years to come to that point in my life, and it was just as important to realize the expectations I had of my husband were not necessarily the same ones he shared for himself.*

Once you come to terms with yourself and your partner and can accept those limitations, you'll find that you live a much more satisfying life. If you are constantly living your life putting your expectations on someone else, you will never find happiness. You will never find the joy in life, and often will find yourself disappointed and feel you've been let down (in your mind).

And the same applies to you. Learn to enjoy your successes and let your failures be lessons to learn from and move forward so that you can strive to do better, be better and live a full life. It's more important to be the best you can be, than to be striving for some unrealistic ideal of perfection or setting goals that can never be reached. Don't waste your time beating up yourself or anyone else with unrealistic expectations. You'll find life will be much more rewarding if you don't.

14

A Lesson Learned Is Never a Wasted Experience

Nothing in life is wasted if you can benefit from it later on. I've had a lot of jobs in my life. Some only lasted a few weeks. Some I thought were a waste of time, only to find out that little job I had one summer working at a jewelry counter laid the foundation for learning to sell baby photographs, which started a whole new career path. *You just never know what's going to help you at some future point. So whatever it is, approach it as if it's the most important thing you will do in your life because, at that moment, it is.*

It took me many years to come to that point in my life, and it was just as important to realize the expectations I had of my husband were not necessarily the same ones he shared for himself.

15

Never Chase a Rat into a Corner, He'll Turn on You

Another way to say this is, always give a rat a gentleman's way out. If you have a confrontation with someone and it looks like a heated discussion that won't be resolved, at least at that time, be willing to give a "gentleman's way out." Make a concession. Acknowledge they may have a good idea or a better way and may deserve further exploration. Unless you are willing to push that person into a corner to where they have no choice but to turn on you, learn to stop before it gets to that point.

I found this principle really applies to working in corporate America. Quite often, I would take one position while another individual would have an extreme opposite position. This situation possibly could escalate into a situation where one or the other would be forced to quit or be fired. Unless you're prepared for this situation, be willing to back off graciously, and save the "life-or-death" battle for something that is worth risking everything. In other words, think rationally. Sometimes letting someone walk away with a small victory will position you for a major victory on a position of greater importance later. Learn to be strategic! This can also apply to a discussion with family members or political views. I'm the black sheep in my family politically. I've learned that sometimes it's just not worth a full-scale war to express my views unless my belief is so strong I'm not willing to compromise my values.

16

When Facing a Crossroad, Measure if the Gain Is Worth the Loss

To continue the line of thinking from the previous chapter, if you're in a situation that tests your resolve, your commitment or conviction, it's time to measure if the gain is worth the loss. What does this mean? It means being responsible for your actions. It may mean putting someone else before your own wants or needs. Sometimes we want to do something so badly and the impulse is so strong, hormones are raging, desire is going full tilt, the need for something is so powerful you're willing to sacrifice anything to get it; this is the time to measure if the gain is really worth the loss...or risk.

Are you willing to sacrifice your job, your spouse, your family, or worse, your life, for the sake of getting something, having something or possessing something? You need to be able to identify if that feeling of love or need or desire is really an obsession and if it's time to back off or risk losing everything you hold dear. Same thing applies to a career. Is your work worth the risk of losing your family? Is the obsession over getting that promotion worth quitting if you don't get it?

17

Never Go Down with a Sinking Ship. Follow the Rats

Loyalty is a wonderful thing. We admire loyalty; we look for loyalty in our friends, lovers, spouses and offspring. Loyalty is one of the most celebrated qualities an individual can possess; I agree.

However, if you're going to be loyal to a fault, meaning you are willing to sacrifice yourself for the sake of loyalty, make sure it's warranted. This means picking those very few important people or issues you are willing to die for such as kids, family, country, a special friend, etc. And for all the rest, you need to know when it's time for survival to kick in and get the hell outta Dodge. It does not mean you should be a rat, or turn on your friends. It means that you need to know yourself well enough to know your boundaries and define, at what point, it's time to step away from a situation or person.

There are some people that will bleed you dry as long as you are willing to give, give and give some more until you are bled out and there's nothing left to give. They'll bleed your time, your money, and eventually, your soul. Don't go there. Don't know how to recognize that point? When you start to feel "used," you've already given too much. You'll recognize the signs when your instincts start to tug on you. End of story.

18

Learning to Say No Is About Knowing Who You Are

It's about boundaries. In other words, know your worth. When I was a young woman, I didn't know what a person meant by boundaries. It took me a long time to figure out something very simple such as things I would or would not do. What was important to me and what wasn't. Seems simple? For those of us who grew up never being allowed to express ourselves, or to have a say in how we define things that were important to us, or to decide what we would or would not do, or to say we did or did not like something, this can be a very difficult journey. It took me a long time to get there. At this point in my life, I say, *don't be afraid to say "No." It's empowering. Remember, a "Yes" is a commitment. Give them wisely.*

When it comes to self-worth, it's about putting a value on you. You are the most important person in your universe. If you don't value yourself, certainly no one else will. When I was 22 I met the wisest man I would ever know. Eventually, we would marry and spend the next 43 years together. And he used to say, "If you take a blue-white diamond and put it in a ten-cent store, people will walk past it or treat it like glass and expect to pay ten dollars. You take that same diamond and put it in the window at Tiffany's, people will pay a fortune for it." You are that blue-white diamond, so treat yourself like a Tiffany.

Screwed, Glued and Tattooed

When I was a young woman, I needed validation...terribly. I'd sell my soul to the devil for words of approval or acceptance. VICTIM!!!!! Whatever reasons my childhood set me up for this are unimportant. However, I was a magnet for every sociopath that walked the earth.

I'm no psychologist and do not profess to be an expert in this area except by experience. After being manipulated, used and let down in an endless Mobius band of repetitive behavior, I finally got wise and began to recognize certain characteristics of sociopathic traits. I encourage those of you who are so inclined, to do more research. For starters, I recommend reading *Type 1 Sociopath* by P. A. Speers. I like this book because she does a great job simplifying what has been very confusing when it comes to personality disorders, and how to deal with people who are more than just difficult people.

What I have come to understand is that the sociopath is a charismatic individual who can charm the pants off of you, make you believe you are the most important person in the world, and then when you have outlived their intrigue or your usefulness, they walk off, with you barely a faint memory.

Many women get sucked in to marrying a man, believing she is the queen in his kingdom, and the minute the tolling of the wedding bells has barely died down, he turns into a monster, usually in the form of emotional abuse and quite often abandoning the relationship, leaving the grieving woman wondering what in the world she did to piss him off. Believe me, it isn't the woman, although he has her thinking she is dumb, stupid, ignorant, dowdy, fat, skinny, and just a plain disappointing low-life and how could such a magnificent specimen of maleness be duped by such a half-wit. And she's left wondering what she could possibly have done to make him loathe her so. What happened to that wonderful prince she married? He never was. It was all an illusion. Hopefully, you don't have to marry one to find out.

Sociopaths are masters of manipulation and deception. Very little they have to say has any basis in truth. Sociopaths manufacture "truth" as needed and are so convincing that they usually have a band of devoted followers, or a string of broken hearts following in their wake, all wondering what the hell happened. They are charming and charismatic and feel almost no remorse for the pain they cause, or seem to be incapable of experiencing shame or guilt. Instead, anything that displeases them is your fault.

The sad thing is if you are a victim craving perpetual approval, you keep licking at boots hoping for some sign of acceptance that will never come, or if lucky, receive an occasional pat on the head to keep you coming back. Stop it! When you feel you've met someone like this, just stop right then. You will never get what you are seeking from these types of individuals and in spite of the powerful attraction, you will lose, lose and lose again.

I once dated a sociopath and he was all of the above. He'd tell me how much he loved me and in the next breath, tell me to take a shower, that I smelled. This form of mental abuse is NOT to be tolerated by anyone. Just RUN!!!

I read a statistic recently that said one in 25 people in the US exhibits some form of sociopathic behavior. Beware. I've focused on men here, but women can be just as sociopathic, using their "friends" to satisfy their need to have power over them, or to use them to do their bidding in some fashion, to serve them in some way. Man or woman, STAY AWAY FROM THESE PEOPLE! Use your instincts instead of your emotions! The need to be loved and appreciated is a powerful force. However, being someone's lapdog or making yourself available to do someone's bidding on any given notice...is no way to find love. If you need this kind of love, GET HELP! GET HEALTHY! Sociopaths seem to know you better than you know yourself, and that's part of their charm. These people can get into your head and you feel so connected, they have you believing they are the only person in the world who understands you. Enough said!

Don't be afraid to say "No." It's empowering. Remember, a "Yes" is a commitment. Give them wisely.

20

I Want You, I Need You,
I Own You

Let's talk a minute about possessiveness. Now this may seem like the ultimate flattery in the beginning of a relationship, but after a couple of years you'll realize they may have excessive control over you, your time, your life, and you let them do it. In the very early stages of a relationship, set the boundaries. If you have a routine of getting together with the girls once a week, don't stop! I know women who have women friends as close as close could be. Enter the possessive man and you never see or hear from her again. She gives away all her power over her own life, and when she finally comes to her senses, it's extremely difficult to take back that power. It almost never works.

You must lay the groundwork when you first start dating...even if you don't want to. Sometimes all you want is to be with "him" every waking moment. BAD IDEA! He'll get used to this and you won't be able to undo it later on when you want to have "lunch with the girls" or take a night class. I personally believe that a lot of problems women have with men becoming stalkers occur because they have given away too much of their power to "him." I had a man do the stalking routine when I was young and I was so flattered I didn't recognize what was happening.

When I was 19 years old, I was pretty naïve and vulnerable. One day I was walking down Ocean Avenue in Carmel, California, when a tall, dark and handsome man crossed the road and walked up to me. He introduced himself and we began talking. He asked if I had time for a cup of coffee and I agreed. We went into a local bakery and began to chat. He was a military officer at Naval Postgraduate School. I was flattered by his attention and after about an hour, he asked if he could call me. I gave him my phone number and that was that.

I didn't hear from him until the following Friday, when he called and asked if I would like to have lunch Saturday. I said yes and we scheduled a place to meet. He was very sophisticated and extremely well educated, spoke several languages, and we had a great time. I was intrigued. About a week later, again on a Friday, he called for another date. We agreed to meet the next day for lunch. After lunch we went for a drive around the famed 17-Mile Drive at Pebble Beach. He was charming and very interesting, worldly, and knocked my socks off. A week later he called again on Friday and we scheduled another lunch date for the next day. We had a great time and he asked if I would be free for dinner some evening. I immediately answered that I would and was thrilled. I realized I was being "courted."

I was living at home with my parents at the time. When I walked through the door after this last date, my mother was waiting for me. She said, "Sharon, we need to talk." I hate that beginning of a conversation. Something bad always seems to follow. The conversation began: "Sharon, I just had an interesting phone call." "Oh?" I replied. "That man you are seeing, I just got off the phone with his wife."

I was stunned! "Did you know he was married?" "Of course not!" I replied. Mom continued, "She seems like a very lovely woman and found your phone number in his jacket pocket." I was dumbstruck. Here I thought he was a perfect gentleman, right out of a romance novel. I was crushed. "You need to stop this before it goes any further!" "Yes, Mom."

I was devastated. Like clockwork, the following Friday he called. I told him I couldn't see him anymore and that I knew he was married. That should have ended it. But it didn't. He kept calling and I knew at times he was following me when I was in my car. I was unnerved and not sure what to do. I told my mother what was going on and she said that I needed to remind him that he had a great deal to lose and if he didn't stop, I would call the Commanding Officer of the Naval Postgraduate School. I did and that was the end of it. Whew! Because it happened early in the relationship, I was lucky. It hadn't evolved into a serious situation and I survived. Unfortunately, not every woman is as lucky as I was.

Love is about having the freedom to be you and allowing each other the freedom to be who they are while being committed.

On the flip side of this, if you are the possessive one, believe me, this is one of the quickest, easiest ways to lose the love of your life. Smothering, owning, possessing, demanding someone to be accountable for every waking minute is a surefire way to have him/her walk, no run, right out the door as fast as possible or create an environment that leads to infidelity. It just never works. So get over it. If he doesn't stay because he WANTS to stay, there's nothing you can do to keep him. Give him his freedom and trust that he'll come back. Keep this thought in mind: You can't lose what you never had.

Love is about having the freedom to be you and allowing each other the freedom to be who they are while being committed.

21

Prince Charming You Are Not

You don't have to be empathic in order to be empathetic. Be empathetic without being compassionate—you can have a sympathetic view of a situation or empathize with a person's plight, but you don't have to experience their pain in order to be a caring or good individual. Learn to care without the emotional attachment or involvement so common to sensitive people. You don't need to absorb pain or try to solve every person's problem or difficulty. Be attentive, willing to listen and provide as much support as you feel you can afford without taking on the other person's problems. Save that for your spouse, partner, kids, etc. *You will experience enough sorrow, pain, disappointment, betrayal and loss in this life all by yourself without taking on the pain of every other person's suffering.* Sounds hard? It's called protecting your inner self.

I've seen people who get sucked into every situation that comes along and by the time they're 30 years old, they look 60 and feel completely drained. Don't let that happen to you. If you are cautious with your emotional giving, when you eventually find that right person in your life, you'll have the reserves within yourself to give of yourself in the right way.

What happens when a casual friend becomes dependent on your friendship and goodwill and their dependency continues to grow, risking your well-being and your family?

It's so easy to own someone else's problems. But you are not "Prince Charming" destined to be their savior. Save that for those who are close at home. Am I preaching? Yeah, guess so. I've just been there firsthand. One important lesson I learned was to know when to draw the line in the sand. It's when it impacts your household or your survival.

There are plenty of organizations and non-profits set up to help people in trouble for spousal abuse, homelessness, etc. If it gets to be a serious problem, refer them to an organization in your area. I've included a list in the back of this book as a place to start. Do NOT put yourself or your family at risk or sacrifice their well-being or yours in a situation like this. Been there, done that.

I have a friend with a wonderful, generous heart who found herself in a situation like this.

My friend, we'll call her Tina, was very generous with a friend, we'll call her Reva. Reva was always in crisis. She lived in a constant state of need. Every day was a struggle for survival and just as she was getting one problem resolved, another would take its place. This went on year after year after year.

One year, property taxes were due on her home and she was struggling to come up with the funds. She had received notice that unless she paid the back taxes, she would lose her home. Many friends over time had come to her aid for this or that, slipping her money for gas, to buy her food or help with a prescription.

One friend, Tina, approached her husband about loaning Reva money to cover property taxes and save her home. These were not rich people and the funds were going to come from Tina's IRA. This was not extra cash lying around. Tina's husband did not want her to do this and they had several heated discussions. In the end, Tina went against her husband's wishes and being the good-hearted person she was, cashed in her IRA and loaned Reva the money on the condition she would sign a promissory note to be paid from the proceeds of the sale of her home. Reva was planning to sell and move to another city.

During the next year, Reva's attitude toward Tina became hostile. Tina couldn't figure it out. What did she do wrong? Reva would avoid calls from Tina and when they finally had a conversation Reva would speak with an attitude of contempt. Tina was hurt and couldn't figure out what the problem was. Finally, Tina, in order to preserve the friendship, sent Reva the promissory note explaining that money was not worth the loss of her friendship. Even with this loving gesture of friendship, when the house sold,

Reva never paid her friend back. As you can imagine, Tina's husband was not happy and it caused problems for them. Not to mention that Tina's retirement fund was now gone.

Reva had serious problems and this was not the only incident of the abuse of friendship.

It's easy to feel compassion for someone in need. It tugs on our heartstrings when we see someone hurt or struggling. Our natural inclination is to help. Just be sure that when you help, you are not risking the lives, safety, survival or general well-being of your household and loved ones. Keep your priorities in line.

People like Reva are negative beings. And negativity breeds negativity. Some people will never change their circumstances. They live in chaos and will attach themselves to anyone willing to be sucked in to their bottomless pit of need.

Stay focused on your goals and self-preservation. Keep negativity OUT of your life. The more you continue to include people like Reva as part of your life, the more their negativity will pull you down.

Remember what I said; *it is unlikely you will bring someone up to your level; more often, they will bring you down to theirs.* And the more you try to, the greater the chances are you will lose. It's better to stop the bleeding early on than to hemorrhage later because, in the end, you will lose.

Pick Your Battles

Not every battle is worth dying for. Pick the ones that are most important to you and then be willing to lose a few only to gain the advantage later on when something for you is really important and is non-negotiable.

You'll be in a better position to negotiate your point. If every battle is fought to the death so to speak, such as with a partner or spouse or boss, then when something really important comes along, they won't know you're serious. They'll just think it's another "issue" and either blow you off because you're just grandstanding again, or fight you to a point of something so serious it could lead to a break-up, loss of job, or even divorce or separation. If you can say to yourself, and your partner, "This is important to me, but I can see it's even more important to you, I'll let this one go," then later, when something for you is REALLY important, you can always say, "Remember when we discussed this issue and I said okay, we'll do it your way? Well, this time, it's non-negotiable for me." Hopefully, they'll realize this issue is really important to you and may be willing to compromise on this point or at least negotiate something that works for both of you.

When in Rome, Do as the Romans

I know I've written a lot about boundaries and self-worth, but there comes a time when you need to respect the beliefs, habits and traditions of others. And if you accept an invitation to someone's home and cannot adapt to their environment, living conditions, or food they serve without them having to completely adjust to your needs, then frankly, you shouldn't go.

When I was 12, my mother, a divorced woman of 29, was dating a handsome man from Southern California. He was a practicing Yogi and vegetarian. He fell madly in love with Mother and about every two months would come to Carmel for a visit. Mother was a fabulous cook and cooked some sort of beef or chicken dish at every meal. It was the way she was raised and we didn't think anything about it. It never occurred to her to cook any differently.

On one visit I asked him why, if he was a vegetarian, he ate meat when he came to our home. He replied, "When in Rome, do as the Romans." Well, being 12, I really didn't understand this and asked him to explain. He did it this way: "I'm a vegetarian by choice, a personal decision. I don't expect anyone to adjust their life to mine, especially when I'm a guest in someone else's home. If I accept an invitation, I accept it on their terms, or I shouldn't be there."

That was one of the most profound statements I've ever heard on this matter and I've never forgotten it. It's about respect. People shouldn't have to conform to your unique beliefs or habits, and you shouldn't try to impose your way of life on others. You either accept their hospitality, or not, the choice is always yours.

Some situations allow "pot luck." You can always let the friend know you have special dietary needs and could you bring a dish. At least you're not saying you won't come. You're letting the person know you don't expect any special treatment but want their friendship. Quite often there will be food that can be eaten and at least you've offered a choice. There's always a gracious way of handling a situation like this and it will be greatly appreciated. This can apply to any situation. Ever had Gefilte fish? Personally, I have a hard time with lamb, but when invited and it's served, I eat and not a word do I utter except to say "Delicious, thank you" and vow never to eat it again! However, I'll admit that on a few occasions, I've been pleasantly surprised, but it's not something I order off a menu.

It is unlikely you will bring someone up to your level; more often, they will bring you down to theirs.

24

Be Assertive Without Being Aggressive, and Know the Difference

When you are faced with a confrontational situation, be direct, say what you mean in a clear and articulate manner, stating your point with conviction and determination without resorting to anger or getting in their face. This is one of the hardest things to learn and your voice can be one of your greatest weapons.

I recommend you practice in front of a mirror. Be aware of how you look, how you express yourself in various situations and what your eyes are doing when you say it. Listen to your voice (I recommend recording these sessions and then playing them back). Learning tonal inflections, listening to how your voice rises or falls at the end of a sentence, can make the difference between winning an argument and coming across as emotional or argumentative. After listening to your recordings, you will find you come across very differently than you think you do. Get to know your voice and the way you say things. You want to be seen as a strong individual who can state a case well without being argumentative, unless it's needed.

Think with your head; learn to control your emotions in a heated discussion and this can move you forward in your career and family situations. You will gain respect for your ability to handle yourself in these situations, whereas as an "in your face" approach can work against you; even if you win the argument, you may lose out on a promotion. And if you do feel anger, learn to control the anger and channel it to give your assertive behavior strength. This is an art if developed and it will give you great strength in the right way. Uncontrolled anger is rage. You don't want to go there.

One more tip: women and children as a rule respond to higher-pitched tones, men respond to lower-pitched tones. If you're trying to make a point when dealing with a man, learn to drop your voice just a little.

25

Fair Only Counts with People Who Are Fair

I grew up in a household where everything had to be fair. Fair? Fair for who? No two people are the same and unless everything is equal, it's probably not fair. The same thing applies in our relationships with other people. If you want to be fair and you're trying to balance things and make sure everyone is "covered," make sure they deserve to be treated fairly. Are they doing fifty percent of the work if you're working on a project together, or have each of you contributed equally to a project, idea or investment? Then it's important to be fair. If one person is doing all the work and the other is taking all the glory, this probably isn't a fair situation unless you don't like to be in the limelight or do the promoting, etc.

It's important to make sure that in any given situation the dynamics and expectations are spelled out clearly. Then when being fair becomes an issue, you have a way to measure it. I have a friend who was in a business situation. They started out working on a project together and were to do the work equally. When the project was all done, my friend was the one who wound up doing a majority of the work and her partner was waiting for her fifty percent of the income after flaking out repeatedly on her portion of the project. Yet my friend felt an obligation to give her the fifty percent of the revenue.

In another situation, I had a friend who was working with an assigned partner on a project to complete their master's degree. Turns out my friend had to complete more than seventy percent of the project, which included the portion her assigned partner was to complete but flaked on. Fortunately, she passed with flying colors. But her partner, who made very little contribution, got the A grade too. Fair? I don't think so. Sometimes it is necessary but that doesn't mean you have to like it, or repeat it.

26

Keep Your Eye on the Donut and Not on the Hole

My stepfather used to say this to me all the time. It's important to take care of details but sometimes you can get so bogged down in the finite details of a situation or problem, you can't see the overall picture or solution, even when the answer is right in front of you. You need to stand back to see the whole donut rather than looking through the donut hole. Quite often, this means stepping back and listening to someone else's point of view. Other times, it's merely walking away from a situation in order to get a fresh perspective. It's easy to fixate on some small aspect of a problem, and you can go round and round with this like a mouse on a treadmill, never seeing the obvious. Oftentimes we can take one small issue and worry it to death, lose sleep, get sweaty palms and fret and stew until we're completely worn out, only to find that in the morning, after a painfully sleepless night, the problem has managed to resolve itself.

27

While Flying at a 30,000-Foot Level, You Better Know Where the Runway Is

There are some people who only see things as a big broad picture. But they cannot see how to implement a plan or they lack the ability to solve problems. They're only looking at things from a 30,000-foot level and fail to see the runway. We need visionaries, planners and implementers. If you have a vision, a grand idea, you had better have a good idea as to how you're going to implement and be able to follow through. I've known people with great ideas and they spend all of their life telling other people what they should or shouldn't do, but never get off the living room couch and do anything themselves. Don't be one of those people. *If you have a great idea, find out what you need to do to plan it out and then figure out how to implement.* If you find out after your due diligence it's not a great idea, be willing to drop it and move on. Just tuck it away for another time. You may find a few years from now you were ahead of your time and it turns out it's now a good idea. And if not, that's okay too. If you have one great idea, chances are you'll have another one. Trust yourself.

28

Money Can't Buy Happiness but It Beats the Hell out of Poverty

First, let me say that money is not evil. There, I've said it. Money is NOT EVIL. Money has no feelings. It doesn't care what you do or don't do with it. What happens with money is up to the people who have it, don't have it, or devise ways to get it. Money serves its master. All money does is set you free and it makes coping with misery a whole lot easier.

If you have a negative attitude toward money, change it. If you don't respect it, it will leave you. I firmly believe having a positive and respectful attitude toward money helps you get it, enjoy it and keep it. Richard used to say, "A fool and his money soon part." These words of wisdom were first published in a rhyme by Thomas Tusser in the sixteenth century. It must have some validity because it's been handed down through all these centuries. Just use your money wisely, don't take it for granted. If it's easy to get, it's just as easy to lose. So take care of it.

Richard always used to put his money in his wallet in order of denomination, beginning with the dollar bills and ending with the twenties or hundreds. I started doing this and found it was an easy way to keep track of how much money I was carrying and spending during the day. A simple little money management trick that can save you a lot. I enjoy and appreciate money. I've been broke and I've been comfortable and believe me, comfortable is a much better place to be and helps you handle difficult situations without the added burden of worrying how you're going to make ends meet. Can you imagine being in the hospital and wondering where the rent money is coming from? We all deal with stress at different times in our lives, and not having to worry about paying the bills is one less thing you need to stress over.

So learn to appreciate what money can do for you, but if you are among the few who have never had to worry about money or where it's coming from, I suggest you take some basic money management courses because there may come a day when you will wish you had. And for heaven's sake, if you have money enjoy it but don't let it rule you.

You will experience enough sorrow, pain, disappointment, betrayal and loss in this life all by yourself without taking on the pain of every other person's suffering.

29

Pass, Play, Hold or Fold

The well-known refrain, "You've got to know when to hold, know when to fold 'em, know when to walk away, know when to run" made famous in the song, "The Gambler," a popular song by Kenny Rogers, expresses the wisdom of a true survivor. When I was a very young woman, I believed in absolute loyalty, sticking by a person or situation without question. My mother used to say I was loyal to a fault. Loyalty is important, as long as you give it wisely. Remember, *loyalty must be earned to be valued and when it's no longer valued, it's time to walk away.* If you don't, chances are you will be discarded like an old shoe. And this applies to personal relationships, friendships, or a job. The ability to know when you are valued and when you are not is the difference between having control over your life and being someone's doormat. Never forget: if you don't value yourself, no one else will.

30

Don't Be Limited by Your Limitations

Doubt in ourselves, a sense of inadequacy or feelings of failure, can keep us from reaching beyond ourselves to even try for something better, to become something more, to be the best we can be. Doubt holds us back. *Doubt is our biggest enemy when it comes to achieving our dreams.* Do not be limited by doubt. Have your dreams. If you recognize you are better at art than at math, then focus on what you are really good at. Identify what you can and can't do and then find the right people to fill in the gaps, and take classes for those things you need to learn.

Winston Churchill became Prime Minister of England at age 62. He also failed the sixth grade and lost every election for public office he ran in.

Teachers of Thomas Edison told him he was too stupid to learn anything. He went on to invent the electric light bulb and countless other inventions.

R.H. Macy failed at every business venture he tried before succeeding. You enjoy the benefits of his success every time you visit the mall and Macy's Department Store.

Steven Spielberg, the director of *JAWS* and other well-known films, was rejected three times from attending his dream school, University of Southern California.

Columbia Pictures allowed their contract with Marilyn Monroe to expire. They told her she wasn't pretty enough or talented enough to be an actress. What did they know?

When you are going for your dream, there is one thing to remember, and mark this well: whoever controls the finances controls the business and that applies to families too! That piece of wisdom came from a CEO of a paint manufacturing company, a wife and mother of two. So if you don't understand how to balance a checkbook, pay your bills or have never managed money, get some training, take a few classes in accounting, and if you are planning to run your own business get training in economics. You better know how to develop a business plan, understand a balance sheet and a profit and loss statement. This is one area of business you do not want to rely on someone else. You may hire others to do the job, but you need to know how to read the reports and manage the results, because *whoever controls the money controls you.* And if you've tried and failed once, try again.

Don't let failure hold you back. *Failure is not personal. It's just a lesson to help you be successful next time.* J.D Rockefeller and Donald Trump both went broke only to come back even stronger. Everyone fails at something sometime. The idea is to figure out what went wrong then try again differently. And keep trying until you get it right. That's the mark of a winner.

Loyalty must be earned to be valued and when it's no longer valued, it's time to walk away.

31

Prince Charming Is Just a Man

Prince Charming Is Just A Man! There's no such thing as the mythical Prince Charming. In our fantasies there is that one special person that comes along and saves us from despair and loneliness to change our life forever. The idea that someone is going to save you is a myth. The only person who can save you is you! If a miracle happens and someone comes into your life, that's a great and wonderful thing, but don't add the burden of expecting someone to be the perfect human who will whisk you away and make life perfect.

Things are going to happen in life. Sometimes bad things or sad things, sometimes wonderful things, some joyous, but be realistic in your expectations and learn to weather the storm if he or she disappoints you at times. Remember, you're not perfect either as much as you would like to believe otherwise. So keep it all in perspective and stay rooted in reality.

32

Never Play Another
Man's Game

Have you ever had someone ask you to pick a card out of a deck, look at it, replace it, then he shuffles a few times and carefully goes through the deck until he finds your card? Hopefully you didn't place a bet. That's playing another man's game. How does that apply to real life? Try the get rich quick schemes. If someone approaches you with a great investment opportunity and you only need a $1,000 to get $10,000 back in a week, run, run, and run some more. This guy will get your $1,000 and you'll have nothing.

We all have a desire for the get rich quick opportunity—scheme is a better word—because that's exactly what it is, a scheme or a con to get you to part with your money. Ask for details, see a balance sheet, and get your attorney to review all documents. If the opportunity is real, the process should be no problem. In the long run, it's better to invest in yourself. Get a license, take a class, start a business, etc.

If you want to gamble, go to Las Vegas. Figure out how much money you can afford to lose, consider it part of your entertainment expense, and have a good time. This is the one time you don't want to have any expectations about getting rich because sure enough you'll get sucked into a game of chance, thinking the odds are in your favor. The odds are ALWAYS in favor of the house. (Remember my words about playing another man's game? This is it.) Personally, I like the shows, but that's me. It's all entertainment so just enjoy it and walk away knowing that by "planned losing," you're a winner. And if you can't afford to lose it, you can't afford to be there. That applies with every investment opportunity as well. People who invest in high-risk stocks play by this rule. It's still gambling! There is risk in every investment. Make sure it's strategic!

33

You Can't Lose What
You Never Had

Anyone above the age of 12 has been jilted one time or another. You can't keep someone from leaving you. People stay in a relationship by choice. Some relationships last a lifetime and others last until they are finished. Sad but true. You can't stop someone from falling out of love with you or leaving you.

Those who are lucky enough to establish a bond in their relationship have a much better chance of weathering the storms through a lifetime together. And whether it lasts or not depends on the people involved. In my experience, it's about two people sharing similar values. I don't care how much you think you love someone; if you don't have a similar value structure as your base in the relationship, the odds are that eventually the two will wind up taking separate roads.

No two people could have been more opposite that Richard and I were. It's like we came from two completely separate worlds with only a shared language holding us together. But at the core of all of that were shared values. From that we forged a bond that carried us through many a storm. Somehow, we always found each other at the center of our universe. Love has its limitations. It's the bond you forge sharing a life together that carries you through the tough times and holds you together. Anyone can experience romance. It's the stuff of soaring emotions, the state of euphoria that transports you into other dimensions. But when you come back to yourself, you better make sure there's earth at your feet.

So before you marry or commit to building a life together, take time to step back and discuss those things that are most important to each of you to find the common ground. If it lasts, wonderful. You are blessed. If it lasts only a few years, you too have been blessed to know love and grow from the experience. One thing I've learned is that people change. Who I was at 20 isn't the person I am today. Somehow Richard and I managed to evolve through the various growth cycles taking place in our lives. This most likely will happen to you.

So right from the start, share your values with each other, write them down and review them every so often to see if you are both on the same page, and if you don't know where to begin, how about with mutual trust, respect and the freedom to be yourself in a relationship. These are the basic components of the successful relationships I've witnessed. Believe me, if you go through this process, you may find your values have changed and you'll agree to part and move on, but at least you may be able to avoid a lot of hurt from infidelity and that horrible sense of loss and betrayal. There are no guarantees in a relationship, but at least you can try to minimize hurting your partner and being hurt.

There are short-term relationships and long-term relationships and each has its value. Something fulfills you at the time for however long it lasts. People come in and out of our lives bringing love, joy, pain and sorrow and lessons. Often, someone comes into our lives for only a short time, but has a lasting lifetime effect.

That happened to me. It wasn't a romantic relationship but still a very important friendship. I lost my mother a few years ago about the same time Richard fell ill, beginning the downward spiral of his life. I met a chaplain who happened to be a client. Through her, I was able to grieve and experience the process of grief and loss that I couldn't show my husband. It was a healing time and when the chaplain was transferred out of the area, I felt a deep loss, a real void, but had our paths not crossed, I'm not sure how I would have gotten through that time of losing my mother. And in the healing that took place, I was free to give more of myself to my husband at a time when he needed me the most and for that, I will always be grateful.

I've had friendships that I was sure would last a lifetime. We traveled together and bonded and shared "Ya Ya Sisterhood" moments. Then they were gone. I'll treasure those friends for what they gave me at the time. They hold a special place in my heart.

Love affairs are just that, affairs. There are only two ways for a love affair to go: evolve into a full commitment or marriage, or eventually part. In the end nothing lasts forever and the world is constantly changing and relationships ebb and flow, and like the waves hitting the beach, they leave little bits of treasure mixed in with debris, but always a beautiful sunset.

Whoever controls the money controls you.

34

Always Carry Extra Batteries

The lesson here is to be prepared for unforeseen obstacles and prepare for the unexpected. You can't control the universe and you can't stop the unexpected from happening, such as a flat tire or an accident on the road. However, you can do the best you can to prevent it from happening, such as checking the air in your tires or the amount of tread. You might not be able to prevent an accident or an event from happening but you can sure reduce the number of accidents that occur and possibly the severity. It could keep you from being stranded in a dark alley some night because you forgot to put air in your tires. Learn to think about what could happen in a situation, then take action to prevent it from happening. It could save your life.

I've learned to do this over the years so I don't even have to concentrate on it, it's just a way of life. For instance, when cooking make sure the handle on the skillet is turned away from your stomach. How many accidents could be prevented by this simple act? Something this simple could prevent you from bumping the handle when you reach for the salt and prevent you from being burned or from a scalding grease spill onto a toddler at your feet. Don't wear long floppy sleeves when cooking; another catastrophe waiting to happen.

Apply this concept of overthinking what could happen to every aspect of your life, and you will reduce your exposure over the course of a lifetime to many preventable accidents, or keep unpleasant situations from occurring.

Apply this same principal to a relationship and it will have a better chance of surviving, but for heaven's sake, don't hen over someone. Just do what you need to without making a production out of it. Think ahead of different possibilities, then do the best you can to prevent it. It's not 100 percent but you will be thankful on many occasions you had the foresight to think ahead.

*So right from the start, share your values
with each other, write them down and review
them every so often to see if you are both on
the same page, and if you don't know where
to begin, how about with mutual trust,
respect and the freedom to be yourself in a
relationship.*

35

Frederick's or Fashion

How many times throughout the years I've heard, "I can take care of myself." The graveyards are full of women who could take care of themselves. Throughout the years women have said they should be able to wear what they want, go where they want, do what they want. This is true, we should, but you have to be willing to accept the consequences. We should live in a world where we as women have the right to wear what we want, whether it's a short skirt, short shorts, halter top, whatever, but be aware the world we live in isn't perfect. And because it isn't perfect, we have to figure out how we can live in it safely.

For instance: Our world is filled with men of integrity. Most men are respectful and have boundaries. They are loving, caring husbands and fathers, boyfriends and employers. Unfortunately, there is a small percentage who will hurt you if given the opportunity. There are people who will do you harm and think that if you are doing this or that, you deserve what's coming to you. They're wrong, of course. But just because they're wrong isn't going to stop them from hurting you. So it's up to you to make sure they don't. If you wave a red flag in front of a bull, you have to accept the bull is going to charge and probably gore you. So the obvious thing to do is, don't wave the red flag and don't go challenging a bull. It's about being responsible for your actions.

I have a friend who attends Bible study with a woman who wants to be a minister. This aspiring minister wears mini-skirts and low-cut tops and one of the men confessed that he was having a hard time with Bible study because he was distracted thinking about her seductive clothes and long legs. Mini-skirts and low-cut tops may be appropriate for certain venues, but church is not one of them. Women need to consider the clothes they are wearing and where they are wearing them. Taking this to the next level. Walking down a street at night wearing a mini-skirt and low-cut top could send the wrong message to a dangerous person lurking in a dark alley. Think about where you are going and what you are doing to prevent something ill-fated from happening to you. And also consider the culture you are living in, or visiting.

Werner Erhard once wrote, "If you stand in the rain you get wet, whether you understand water or not." In other words, things can happen, good or bad, if you put yourself out there, even if you don't understand why it happens. You don't have to understand WHY something happens to you; you just have to know how to keep it from happening or at least reduce the odds. Recognize there are certain consequences to your actions and be willing to accept the responsibility for those actions. If you know what the potential of those actions is, you can prevent or at least reduce the consequences.

There is a basic law of physics: for every action, there is an equal and opposite reaction. Think about what you do before you become a victim of your own behavior. It's not your fault we live in a society that produces sick behavior in a few, but it's the few you have to protect yourself against. So do it.

We should live in a world where we as women have the right to wear what we want and be what we want. But be aware of the world we live in, be aware of your surroundings, and know you have to be responsible for your own safety. End of story!

36

If You Fill Your Heart, You Feed Your Soul

Confucius said, "Choose a job you love, and you'll never have to work a day in your life." Truer words were never spoken. If you love what you do, it is said it will extend your life because you are being fulfilled. And if your job doesn't do it, and you're just working to live, then find your bliss in another way. Survival comes first, always. *Finding your bliss can make survival seem like a joyous journey.* It doesn't matter how busy you are or what you are doing, whether you're raising a family, working two jobs or whatever; take time out to find that one thing in your life that feeds your soul. You don't have to be good at it; it's the act of doing that fills you with a sense of well-being. *And a strange thing happens along the way when you love what you are doing: you become good at it.*

If you are lucky enough to find bliss through your career, so much the better. It could be reading books, writing poetry, painting a picture, walking your dog on the beach, holding a child in your arms or running a company or a country...it's the one thing you give yourself every day, or at least once a week, that makes you feel at one with the universe.

For you young women, if you are career minded, then find your bliss in a career. If you like children, then work with children. If you enjoy building things, then build. If you're in a job to earn a living but it's not your bliss, then find the hobby or activity which fills the need. But find it.

"If you find your bliss, great things can happen" -Peggi Speers.

37

Take Time for Yourself Today as Tomorrow May Never Come

We all need time to ourselves. If you don't have a calendar, get one. Schedule time just like any dental or doctor's appointment. Put it in your cell phone. It's just as important to schedule time for yourself as it is to have dinner with your husband or turn in a term paper for school. YOU ARE IMPORTANT TOO. Now is the time to learn it before you reach the tender age of 80 and get to wondering what the heck happened to your life. By scheduling time for yourself you'll have time, energy and the mindset to confront the daily demands, all those obligations you need to meet and patience when you need it.

You may be thinking, how do I do this? Well, it's simple. Be selfish. *If you can schedule time for a "HOT DATE," you can schedule time for yourself.* It's about priorities, and your number one priority should be you. Because if you don't take care of yourself first, you won't have anything left to give to anyone else. So ladies, kick guilt out! GUILT DOESN'T LIVE HERE ANYMORE.

38

Anger Versus Revenge

It's good to get angry rather than holding it in. You never want to bottle up anger because it can make you sick. So it's good to state why you're angry, find a constructive way to express it and then let it go and move on.

Revenge is a whole other subject. The need for revenge is a sickness. Confucius said, "Before you embark on a journey of revenge, dig two graves." At some point in all our lives, we have had or will experience the desire for revenge. My suggestion is to think about it, write it down or find some positive way to express it then release it. If you write it down, tear up the paper and burn it, then be done with it. I've known people to let anger fester like a pustulous wound, who plotted revenge waiting for just that right moment to strike. Their lives were consumed with the need for revenge and this usually ended in disaster or their own illness. And quite often, after the preemptive strike was completed, it was a letdown. The feeling of elation and victory just wasn't there. It wasn't worth all the time of planning and plotting to have it all come plummeting down to earth. The gain wasn't worth the effort.

You have too much to do, too much to accomplish in life, and your life is much too valuable to waste time on the wrongs and ills of all the stupid rotten thoughtless acts of betrayal or some other type of thoughtless self-absorbed behavior exhibited by someone else to wallow in a cesspool of anger and self-destruction. Think it, write it, and be done with it.

39

No Matter Your Goal, Make the Journey as Part Of the Process

Goals are great, but don't forget to enjoy the journey. We all have goals in life but sometimes we get so focused on the goal that we lose all the joy in the process of achieving the goal. Goals can change and sometimes you may achieve a goal only to find out it isn't enough or it isn't what you want after all. But if the journey has been part of the process, you can come away still feeling a sense of accomplishment and enjoy the lessons learned along the way and figure out what you really want to do.

It's like taking a trip across country. You start out in San Francisco and your goal is New York, but you discover along the way after a short stopover that Salt Lake City offers the same opportunities you were looking for in New York City, and you decide to stay in Salt Lake City. Life is like that. You may be so focused on the goal of reaching New York City you would drive right through Salt Lake City missing out on a perfect job opportunity or meeting that perfect partner standing at the cash register as you stopped for gas. Be open to the detours in life as they may offer many opportunities that otherwise might be missed.

I know a woman who was a professional jazz singer. She was from New York City and had bookings all across the country. She arrived in Monterey, California, by car scheduled to sing at a well-known nightclub. As she drove into the parking lot, a car was backing out and they had a collision. Both drivers got out of their cars and started yelling at each other. Turns out, he was her accompanist during her stay at the nightclub. Two weeks later they were married. She never returned to New York except for short visits from time to time. They remained married over 40 years until his death.

40

Personal Integrity, Honor and Trust

When you say you will do something, do it. Don't make a commitment unless you are prepared to follow through. Most of us are seeking relationships of great trust. You must never forget in order to have trust you must earn trust. It goes both ways. There is nothing that hurts more than the betrayal of trust. It's devastating. But when it comes to trust, you only have control over your own behavior and no one else's. So that's where you begin.

If through the course of your lifetime, someone betrays you, it's going to hurt like hell and don't think you're going to escape it. It happens to everyone at some point in time. Just because someone betrays you doesn't mean you stop trusting or worse, become spiteful and eventually become the very thing you hate. Keep and protect your personal integrity, don't let anyone damage who you are, and be on guard to ensure your personal integrity isn't used against you. *Give your trust sparingly and only to those who have earned it.* When a person breaks your trust, you owe them nothing so walk away as fast as you can and don't look back.

What about second chances? Hmm. Be careful with this one. Anyone can make a mistake. But if your boyfriend has cheated on you and has a history of cheating on his girlfriends, he's going to cheat again. Don't make the mistake of thinking you're the "special one" in his life. It just ain't so. You're one in a long line of wimpy women who keep falling for his line of BS. So stop and get out.

On the other hand, if you're married with a couple of kids and he's never cheated on you before, this may be something to consider. You have to think about this carefully but try to work to get to the heart of the problem. There was a movie a few years ago with Billy Crystal and Bruno Kirby titled *When Harry Met Sally*. There is a scene when Crystal's character is devastated when he learns that his wife is having an affair. Kirby's character pops up and says, "Marriages don't break up on account of infidelity. It's just a symptom that something else is wrong." Crystal's response is, "Yeah, but that symptom is f___king my wife."

In a situation like this, you have to consider all the possibilities. You don't want to set yourself up as a doormat for your husband's indiscretions, but neither do you want to blow a marriage that is salvageable if both parties are willing to work at it. I've known couples who have survived infidelity to become the strongest relationships I've ever seen, lasting 40 and 50 years. Take it on a case-by-case basis considering the people involved.

Finding your bliss can make survival seem like a joyous journey. And a strange thing happens along the way when you love what you are doing: you become good at it.

41

Fake It 'Til You Make It

This is a saying we used when I first started out in sales. I was so nervous about not knowing what I was talking about that I was scared to say anything, until I heard, "Fake it 'til you make it." And through the course of my lifetime I've used this approach to get me through many awkward situations.

This does not mean lie. If you don't know something, say so and you'll get an answer. But for goodness' sake, say it with confidence. Have you ever walked into a room and not known anyone? Did you feel self-conscious or insecure? That's a common reaction. The badass woman may feel these things too but no one will know it because she has an air of confidence like the room is HERS! She owns it.

I heard a story about the filming of the movie *The Big Sleep.* As the story goes there is a scene where Lauren Bacall walks down a great hall to meet Bogie and her sister at the front door. She was unsure what to do with her hands as she walked this lengthy passage with the camera focused on her the whole time. Bogie gave her some great advice. "Walk with purpose," he told her, and she did. It's a memorable scene and that's what I recommend to you. *Walk with purpose. Approach life with purpose, enter a room with purpose, and it's just a matter of time before people are coming over and talking to you.* Or, you'll walk over and make a first introduction: "Hi, I'm Sharon Law Tucker, who are you?"

It's that simple. Don't worry if you run out of things to say, just politely excuse yourself and move on to the next introduction. It's all about confidence! You don't fear rejection and more importantly, you don't feel rejected. You'll either connect with someone or you won't. Don't dwell on it.

42

You're Only as Strong as Your Weakest Link

Think about this for a minute. *No matter how capable or intelligent you are, whatever weaknesses you have or what areas you are most vulnerable, that is how strong you really are.* There are things you may not be able to change about yourself, but you can learn to guard your vulnerabilities and overcome your weaknesses by capitalizing on your strengths.

I was painfully shy as a young woman. And no matter how well I dressed or did my makeup and hair, no matter how well I entered a room, my shyness was most definitely my weakest link. I would get tongue-tied just trying to introduce myself. Fortunately, Richard worked with me over and over until I was able to not only introduce myself but deliver sales

123

presentations. Now, years later, I am able to stand in front of a room full of people and very comfortably run meetings and speak from the hip. It's show time!

Have you ever known someone who seems to have everything going for them only to self-sabotage and make the same mistakes repeatedly? I don't care how great someone is, or how smart or talented, if they have a drinking problem, a drug problem or if they let their egos get in the way of being employable, that's who they are and that's where they will stay unless they take positive steps to make serious changes. We need to learn to recognize our weaknesses whatever they may be so we can strengthen them or learn to manage them so we are not held back by them.

I have a friend who is dyslexic. She learned to overcome her reading difficulties by listening and developing her memory. She's a straight A student and brilliant. While she lives with her dyslexia every day, she's learned to overcome her weakness and developed other skills in the process. Some of the biggest corporations in the country are run by people with dyslexia. It hasn't held them back because they found a way to deal with it. If you have something you perceive to be a weakness or shortcoming, find a way to overcome it. In the long run, you could make it work to your advantage

Give your trust sparingly and only to those who have earned it.

43

Manage Your Life as You Manage Your Money

It's all about educating people to value you as much as they value themselves. Start with the small stuff, such as scheduling your time, and then build from there. When people realize you're scheduling time for them, when they begin to think, "I am important to her because she is making time for me," they'll start respecting you as well as your time and stop taking you for granted. If you make yourself too accessible, then you must not have anything more important to do. *If you respect your time, others will too.*

Walk with purpose. Approach life with purpose, enter a room with purpose, and it's just a matter of time before people are coming over and talking to you.

44

A Hard Head Makes a Soft Ass

This old Southern expression says a lot in its simplicity. If you don't listen to those who are wiser than you, you may have to suffer the consequences of experiencing some difficulty. Sometimes that can be a very painful lesson. Keep your mind open and listen to those who have something to teach you and you'll make your life a lot easier by capitalizing on the experience of those who have paid the price.

Being self-sufficient and self-reliant is a great thing, a trait to be admired. But don't be so bull-headed you cancel yourself out learning from the wisdom and experience of others. As Richard used to say, "Those who do not listen must feel."

No matter how capable or intelligent you are, whatever weaknesses you have or what areas you are most vulnerable, that is how strong you really are.

45

Charity Starts at Home

I'm all for helping people who need help, especially those who help themselves. I've been a volunteer and on the board of seven non-profits over the years, done fundraising, and am currently working for a foundation where I've been employed for eight years. With all that being said, I believe you have to take care of yourself and family first. As Richard often said, charity starts at home.

When I was in my early twenties, I was making very little money at the time and barely squeaked by between paychecks. I had just come out of a grocery store and was walking toward my car when a young man came up to me. This was in the late sixties and the young man was dressed in the typical hippie fashion. He must have known I was a soft touch because he gave me the story about how he had just run out of gas and would I give him a couple of bucks to buy some. All I had was a five-dollar bill to get me to payday, which was five days away. You guessed it! I gave him the five. For 30 seconds I felt really good about helping someone until it sunk in that I didn't have money to buy gas to get to work until payday a week away.

About opening your home up to those in need...be very careful here. You can start out thinking that this person just needs a place for a week or so and it ends up turning into months or even years. Been there, done that. And it rarely ends well. I'm not saying don't do it; I'm just saying be careful. We all need a helping hand at some point in our lives, but there are those who will abuse your kindness and use it against you for as long as you're willing to give it. Then there are those who will accept your help and use it as the boost they need to move forward, get that new job, start school, or whatever goal they have. And that's what you want.

46

Mountains Are Meant to Be Climbed

Hardships can mold success. Like forging steel by anvil and fire into a fine-edged sword, having to experience hardships can help you develop survival skills, analytical thinking and other abilities as well as the drive and commitment to turn your life around. Great things have happened by people who have come from poverty and hardships because they had the drive and motivation to change their lives.

One such man was Harry Gordon Selfridge. Harry was an American who came from extreme poverty who went to London and founded the Selfridge Department Store. In 1909 this was a big deal when he opened the first store in Britain where people of all classes shopped together and he introduced the first Bargain Basement shopping floor. Although Harry lost his personal fortune (he squandered it through gambling and general mismanagement), in 2012 the Selfridge store was the highest-earning retail store in the world.

Harry was a man with a vision. Whatever difficulties we experience, we do have the potential to turn things around. It just takes a vision, a plan and the desire to implement.

47

A BadAss Woman Is Never Mediocre, She Lives Life Large

This has nothing to do with how much money you have, how successful you are or how big your house is. It's a state of mind. It's the thought behind what you are doing that matters. It's being able to enjoy life each and every day even in the face of adversity.

Richard often said, "You eat life or life eats you." Don't be afraid to stretch yourself, try new things, etc., and go at it with a positive attitude.

And don't forget to take time to enjoy the world around you; the small blessings that are right in front of you transform a mediocre existence into a rich, full life. Even if you're living on pennies a day, the world is full of free things to enjoy such as a walk on the beach, laughing with friends, playing with your kids, the aroma of flowers in your garden, the sound of birds nesting in trees, doing something in a different way. Feed your senses so that nothing is lost and at the end of the day, there are no regrets, no if only I had done this or that. Live life to the fullest and on your terms, making the most out of each and every day.

Richard told me a story. There have been many different versions but this one is one that stays with me.

"A man came across three carpenters who were building a tall building. The man asked the first carpenter what he was building and he replied, 'It's just a big building and I'm tired and I'll be glad when it's finished.' The man continued around the corner and came to the second carpenter. When asked what he was building, the second carpenter replied, 'I'm building a great big church. It's a lot of work but it will be nice when it's done.' The man continued on and came to the third carpenter. When the man asked what he was building, the third carpenter stood back, looked up at the structure, spread his arms wide and replied, 'I'm building a magnificent cathedral. People from all around will be able to come here to worship and praise God.' All three carpenters were building the same building but each had a very different perspective as to what they were doing."

It's all about your attitude and how you approach what you are doing, not the task itself, that determines what you get out of life.

It's all about educating people to value you as much as they value themselves. If you respect your time, others will too.

Final Thoughts

The great humorist Erma Bombeck wrote, "If life is just a bowl of cherries, why did I get all the pits?" Pits grow into trees and trees bear luscious fruit. It's up to you to figure out if you're going to settle for the pits or enjoy the cherries. Personally, I prefer living a badass life. Cherries Jubilee anyone?

Notes

Resources

Homeless Services:
- Homeless Service Centers
- YWCA

Alcoholism Support:
- Alcoholics Anonymous
- Al Anon – for friends and family of alcoholics
- Co-Dependency Anonymous – for spouses

Spousal Abuse Support Services
- Women's Outreach Center

Financial Literacy
- Enchantedlearning.com – online service explains the basics of budgets and planning for the future.
- Wells Fargo and Bank of America are resources to help you handle your personal finances. Check on the internet for additional resources.

- Debt.org is a great source to help understand and manage debt. Student information Web pages offer information regarding financial aid, understanding budgeting, and navigating student debt repayment.
- Money-wise.org is a national financial literacy partnership of Consumer Action and Capital One, and is the first program of its kind to combine free, multilingual financial education materials, curricula, and teaching aids with regional meetings and roundtables to train community-based organization staff so that consumers at all income levels and walks of life can be reached.

Acknowledgments

Many thanks to the following: Therese Soares, my special young friend who inspired the writing of this book and gave it its title; Peggi Speers, the owl in my life whose attention to detail kept me focused and the countless hours of proofing, feedback and encouragement, and for the unwavering belief I would and could write long before I did; Sheila Shaw for her vast technical help, cover design, and web design, who never ceases to dazzle me with her amazing ideas and talent and personal commitment to getting this book published; my sister, Rebecca D. Law, who has been there for me through thick and thin; my dear friend Genevieve Demings for so many years of friendship and unconditional love; the Keller family for accepting me into their home as one of them and calling me Auntie

Sharon; Judy Overeiner who, for over 20 years, has been a special friend, near and far; Maria Valentin, Jurgen Sottung, and Scarlett Rogers for countless hours of love, friendship and great conversations; Suzanne Hendrick, friend and neighbor, who shared the experience of loss with me, and for all the help and love from Frank and Barbara Strehlitz, Sal and Ada Lucido and Louie Darwin and Edith Law, for their love and support through really difficult times. And most of all, to Richard, my badass husband whose wisdom made this book possible.

Made in the
USA
Columbia, SC